Unbelievable Pictures and Facts About Jamaica

By: Olivia Greenwood

Introduction

Jamaica is a Caribbean island, filled with beautiful mountains and magnificent rainforests. Today we will be learning all about wonderful Jamaica. We hope you enjoy learning all these new and interesting facts.

Are there any beaches to visit in Jamaica?

If you enjoy going to the beach then you may really love Jamaica. You will find plenty of different beaches all over Jamaica.

Will you find any rivers in Jamaica?

The answer is a big yes. There are many rivers all over Jamaica. The longest river is known as the Black River.

Which language do people speak?

In Jamaica, the majority of people speak English. They do speak other languages in Jamaica too.

How many years on average do people in Jamaica live for?

On average the people in Jamaica have very long lifespans. Men live up until 78 years of age on average. Women, on the other hand, live up until 74 years of age.

Does Jamaica have a national tree?

The answer is a big yes. The tree which is considered to be the national tree of Jamaica is called the Blue Mahoe.

Which sport do people love the most in Jamaica?

Can you guess which sport is the most popular in Jamaica? The sport which is the most popular is cricket.

Which religion is practiced the most in Jamaica?

The religion which is practiced the most in Jamaica is Christianity.

Do any well-known people come from Jamaica?

Over the years there have been many famous people who have come from Jamaica. One of the most famous is Bob Marley.

What types of food do people eat in Jamaica?

People eat all sorts of food in Jamaica. Some of the most popular dishes include curried goat and saltfish.

Is Jamaica a popular place to come and visit?

Jamaica has always been a really popular place to come and visit. Unfortunately over the years, it has become quite dangerous for tourists and for this reason, fewer tourists visit Jamaica.

What is the tallest point in the country called?

If you go to Jamaica and you are looking for the highest peak, you will find it at Blue Mountain Peak.

Which financial currency do they use?

If you wish to buy things in Jamaica it may be useful to learn which financial currency they use. The financial currency which they use in Jamaica is the Jamaican Dollar.

What is the population size in Jamaica?

Jamaica is home to nearly 3 million people. Each and every single year the population amount grows.

Which is the capital city?

The name of the capital city is Kingston. This has been a capital city since 1872.

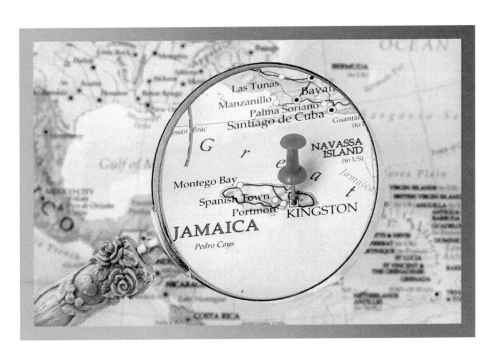

Will you find many animals in Jamaica?

In Jamaica, they have many animals. If you look closely enough you may even spot an animal or two that is totally unique and can only be found in Jamaica.

What type of weather do they experience in Jamaica?

Jamaica experiences all sorts of different weather conditions. During the summer months, it has a tendency to get extremely hot. Unfortunately, earthquakes and hurricanes occur in Jamaica.

Will you find any museums in Jamaica?

If you like visiting museums, then you will really enjoy Jamaica. There are tons of interesting museums to visit all over Jamaica.

Is it safe to travel in Jamaica?

Unfortunately, over the years, it has become quite unsafe to travel in Jamaica. However, there are still some good parts which are safer than others.

What type of landscape does Jamaica have?

Jamaica has a really beautiful landscape. It is an island which is surrounded by mountains, valleys, rainforests, and coastal plains.

Where in the world will you find Jamaica?

Jamaica can be found far away in the Caribbean islands. It is situated on the Carribean sea.

Made in United States
North Haven, CT
02 May 2023

36112835R00024